The Chronicles of the Ancient Wizard of Avalon

To Mrs Angela and all my good friends at the Temple Bar in Dublin Ireland, Sir John L. Greene The 2nd

Sir Uriel Enoch Sinclair

Spread the news

HUDSON REGIONAL LIBRARY

Copyright © 2019 Sir Uriel Enoch Sinclair
All rights reserved
First Edition

PAGE PUBLISHING, INC.
New York, NY

First originally published by Page Publishing, Inc. 2019

ISBN 978-1-64462-154-7 (Paperback)
ISBN 978-1-64462-155-4 (Digital)

Printed in the United States of America

I n the year of our Lord AD 562, there was a young woman named Alyssa giving birth to a precious baby boy. He was the seventh son, born on the seventh day of the seventh month from a royal family in despair. He would become the end of bloodshed and war and the beginning of an era of peace when life becomes fair. Education was only for the rich, change became a reality for a witch, and college institutions had a lease. Woe unto his enemies of state for this young boy was the heir to the throne and destined to be king. This is his story unto his coronation when the church bells ring. The witnesses of his birth were only his brothers and his aunt Denise.

It has been given to me on this day of prophecy a story of a young boy whom shall one day be king of the wizards of Avalon on a beautiful spring morning as the morning birds sing. Alyssa had given birth to a seven-pound baby boy, born on July 7, AD 562. He was a beautiful and handsome son of the king of the Isle of Anglesey, King William III. The young boy's name was Bill. His brothers were Simon, the oldest brother, Philip and Ralph, the second and third oldest brothers, George and Peter were the fourth- and fifth-oldest brothers, then there was John. He was the youngest brother of the royal family until now. His father, King William, and his army were currently at war with France.

All six brothers were sent to the finest school in Europe, the University of Cambridge. Bill grew up inside the castle walls with his pet dog, Amos. John and his brothers were gone each year, living in the dorms of their school. Simon was studying to be a herbalist and a doctor. Philip was studying to be a lawyer. Ralph was studying to be an architect. George and Peter were studying to be college professors. John was studying to be a scholar, a poet, a musician, a writer, and a shaman. The difference in the geographic location of the brothers education was that the other six brothers went to the same school, Cambridge University in Trinity Lane, Cambridge CB2 1TN, United Kingdom, and Bill, the youngest brother, was home-schooled ever since the day he was born. He was still studying basic academics because he was still in elementary school.

A young lad, strong and bold, healthy as a Clydesdale horse who never gave up and never would fold. Bill wasn't like the rest of his brothers. He knew what he wanted, and he knew what he wanted to be. He never gave up, and he never gave in while living in a cruel noncaring world of bloodshed and sin. Bill and John grew up together being the closest of brothers over all the rest. After John and the other older brothers graduated college, everything changed. The boys became men, looking for some young female hens. They had gone through puberty, and their hormones had changed. They didn't want to live their lives poor, lonely, sick, and sad, living lives like dying dogs with mange. So when John, Simon, Philip, Ralph, George, and Peter all came home from college, their father, King William III, had just come home with his army after having won long battle between England and France.

Sir King William was tired, hungry, and not in a good mood. Although they won the war, he had lost two hundred good men in the northern territory before it was over. Their father needed some time alone with their mother, Queen Alyssa, to recuperate from the long journey. One week went by, and William felt better. He was fed and rested. He was no longer cold, tired, hungry, and depressed. He no longer felt threatened or tested. The brothers came to spend time with their father. This gave him encouragement and made him feel better. They helped him to his throne as he read his ambassador's letters. Apparently, France wanted a truce and to meet with the heads of state to negotiate a peace treaty lest more soldiers meet their fate. King William wasn't sure. He had been betrayed before and didn't want to put himself, his people, or his country what they went through before.

He thought about it, and this is what he said: "If France wants a truce by negotiating a peace treaty, this is what they will have to do. France is going to have to prove their trust worthiness to establish peace like they knew. The king of France will have to sacrifice some weapons and land. Both England and France would have to exchange something they love the most as an ingenious plan."

Sir King William III set up a diplomatic meeting with the heads of state between France and England. King William and his army were already half worn out from the last war, where so many men died. So William was ready to negotiate peace between both countries. So the heads of state set up the meeting between England and France at the House of Commons one week from the day it was planned. Either the peace treaty would go successfully, or it would be damned.

In the meantime, the boys needed rest and relaxation, companionship, and recreation. It was therapeutically vital for their human mental stability. While the whole royal family were waiting for the peace treaty meeting between their father, the king of France, and the heads of state, Sir William, Alyssa, and their sons went on vacation to the island of Bimini. International archaeological rumors has it that the Ancient Lost City of Atlantis lies somewhere at the bottom of the Atlantic Ocean. That it stretches from the southern tip of Africa off the coast of Bimini and goes all the way to the southern tip of Florida of the United Colonies. This was in the unexplored version of what would later become the United States of America after the ending of British Parliament rule. Atlantis continued to go from Florida to the southwestern coast of Cuba, which was owned by the king of Spain, back to the southern tip of Africa again. The royal family wanted to explore the island of Bimini and snorkel underwater to try to see if they could spot the city themselves.

Sir William and the boys arrived by boat to the island of Bimini and were amazed at its beauty. There were tall beautiful coconut trees, pineapple trees, kiwi, and wild berries. There were also banana trees and millions of monkeys. However, as beautiful as the island was with walruses, seals, and crabs everywhere. There were hidden dangers on the island as well. There were giant tarantula spiders, millions of giant ants, and some of the most poisonous snakes on earth on the island of Bimini. They were puff adders, cottonmouth moccasins, as well as the black and green mambas. So the royal family carefully explored the island, prospecting for ancient relics and gold.

The royal family's vacation was very therapeutic and bonded them all together in a life that was usually in despair. When the king is at war fighting other foreign armies with his army, his wife is usually at the castle, worrying half to death about whether or not her husband is going to come home alive, let alone with all his limbs. Finally, for the first time in a whole year, the queen and her children were able to spend time with her husband and father of her children. Their moods were great. It is better at any time to still be alive even when the timing is a bit late. Some of his warriors didn't get to go on vacation after fighting the war and meeting of their fates. The royal family was thankful that they were still alive and spending quality time together on a tropical island paradise. They were absorbing the beautiful sites, atmosphere and watching the ocean tide rise. The next morning came, and the family woke up out of their nice little sleeps. Bill brought some turtle eggs back to the camp. John gigged some fish. The other brothers brought back firewood as William prepared some coffee for the fire. Alyssa cleaned the fish and made bowls out of cut-up coconut shells and made forks out of tree limbs.

Once William got the fire started, he put the metal coffeepot in the fire. Alyssa made and ran homemade skewer spit rods for cooking and rotissering the meat over the fire after the coffee was made. The royal family ate their morning tropical breakfast and drank British coffee and had tea with crumpets. After waiting three hours to digest their food and beverage, they went swimming and snorkeled thirty feet to the bottom of Bimini's Atlantic Ocean floor. They swam for two hours, looking for the city with no avail. However, as soon as they got tired of swimming, *voila*! The youngest brother found the city!

Apparently, it was located on the other side of the coast. They explored the city for another hour until they were too tired to swim or boast. The family went back to camp, gathered more firewood and herbal ingredients to make more mosquito repellent. They even did more hunting and fishing for food. They went to the fresh water springs for clean, edible, consumable water. When the family was done with their camp chores, they called it a night and went to bed till the crack of dawn. Morning came as night disappeared. The royal family woke up early to get an early start on getting back to the ship to travel back home. William and his wife packed all the family's bags while the boys took turns loading them back on the little skiff boat. They rowed back to the mother ship and transferred the bags and cargo onto the ship. When they were done, they used a manual winch to hoist the little dingy skiff boat onto the side of the ship. Once again, they were underway on a course set to the coordinates of latitude 55.3781 degrees north and longitude 3.4360 degrees west toward the mother country they call home.

As they headed back home, British Parliament would never be the same. Instead of being tired, stressed out, and depressed all the time, the royal family would go home with a whole new clean slate mentally, spiritually, and socially. They would handle all business of social, political, and economical interest and make England a better place to live. The real trick would be convincing disbelieving, hateful nations which were always accustomed to living their lives in uncertainty, fear, with a lack of trust while whispering hints of a possible revolution. Woe unto he, she, or any group preaching a possible attempt to take over the British Parliament for they would be tried for high treason and executed before the people of England.

When the family arrived back home, William went to the House of Commons and summoned his administration and cabinet members of the House for a business and political meeting. Sir King William wanted to decide through the House if trusting France with a peace treaty would be a wise or foolish decision. He waited, and fifteen minutes later, all the members showed up. Once they all sat down and got the small business affairs of local business out of the way, Sir King William stood up and spoke. He said, "We must learn from all the mistakes of our forefathers from the past. Trust is one of the biggest yet most controversial word that doesn't always last. For if we trust just any other countries at their word and war breaks out, all the peace treaties in the world will never change anything. Gentlemen, we must think clearly about this proposal before we make a decision to just trust the political leaders of France with their words at face value. We as a family, a race, and as a country must make ingenious wise decisions in order to protect us all from the isms and dictatorships of other countries of this whole world. United we stand, but divided we fall!" At that moment, all the members of the House stood up and said, "Here! Here!"

Sir Winston Sinclair stood up and said, "Pardon me if I do say, Sir. What guarantee do we have that we can trust France at their word even with a signed peace treaty?"

Sir Buckley of the House of Bradley stood up and said, "If we had some kind of assurance that we as a nation can trust France, we, the honorable members of the House, would feel better about trusting a country our country has been at war with on and off for over seven generations now. If we only had some kind of assurance policy that France wouldn't break the treaty between both countries."

He continued with, "We would vote right now to establish a treaty between both countries."

Sir King William stood up and said, "Well, I know that the king of France is willing to grant the House of Commons one-fourth of their land deeds for the purpose of building schools for the children to learn necessary education. I also know that France is willing to give five hundred thousand pounds in sterling toward the reestablishment of creating jobs, transportation, and housing for the poor and homeless of Great Britain. If France will give our navy access to France's territorial waters to ensure the safety of our import/export merchant ships for the future continuing existence and sake of international world trade. If they stop invading our allies, we will sign the new peace treaty under the new constitution. This will be signed by the whole European Union, ensuring that France will not breach the treaty before the new year even begins. By the time all the other allies of England signs the new constitution and peace treaty between England and France, if France breaks the new treaty and constitution, all of England's allies alone will utterly destroy France permanently. France will cease to exist as a nation and a people. England will ultimately rule this whole world through unification of the European Union of all of England's allies unto the new world of peace."

After Sir King William of Great Britain finished speaking, the ambassadors of France agreed. Germany, Ireland, Scotland, Poland, Switzerland, Australia, Russia, and the United Colonies all agreed and signed the constitution and peace treaty between England and France. This put a final end to a war between all the countries of Europe for seven hundred years. Mainly, the godforsaken war between England and France for many generations before was finished.

After all the countries of the European Union signed the new constitution and treaty of newly established peace, all the world leaders and ambassadors of all the countries involved ate dinner and drank wine together. They later shook each other's hands and parted ways. After a very long peace talk of negotiations and considerable amounts of thought, Sir King William III was satisfied with the talks and decided to go home to his family. Then he prepared his business according to his daily agenda for the following business day.

The boys were in their beds sleeping, and the queen had William's supper simmering to stay warm over some hot coals of the fireplace. The queen said, "Welcome home, my beloved husband. For your dinner is ready and awaiting your presence."

Sir William said, "Thank you, my queen. For I had a long day at work. The political meeting went longer than I thought it would. Now I am so tired and hungry, that I feel like I am going to pass out. Please don't feel bad if I do."

Alyssa said, "You know me better than that, my beloved husband. I would never be offended by you, my love."

William ate his dinner and went to bed.

The next morning the family woke up bright and early. It was the weekend, and the boys had plans to go out with their friends and have fun. Alyssa had an appointment with the Women's Fashion Club. William had another meeting with the House of Commons about the signed declaration of a peace treaty. It was to be elaborated on to determine if moving forward on to the next piece of business would be a wise thing to do or if trusting France was even wise at all. Allysa went to her appointment, and William went to his. All the boys except two went out with their friends.

They went mountain climbing and swimming with their girlfriends. Bill and John stayed at home doing homework because they had exams Monday morning. When they were done with their homework, they left to go for a walk. They walked for miles through forests and crop fields until they reached a location called Salisbury Plain. All of a sudden, they stopped in their tracks. They were staring at the biggest, most beautiful, scariest, yet most mysterious place in Britain. This place was now known as Stonehenge. They paused in awe for a while, then proceeded to walk the whole henge, amazed at the size and magnificence of the structure itself. They were marveled at the precision and how square level and plumb it was. They were amazed at the architectural skill and years of experience it must have taken to build the henge. The boys were so marveled and amazed at what they were seeing. They didn't want to leave.

Out of nowhere, a tall old man with a long white beard, wearing a long white garment appeared right in front of them. He said, "Greetings, young masters. I am a voice from the past long ago. An ancient time from whence mankind of today does not know."

The boys said, "Greetings, for we are the—"

The old man interrupted them, saying, "The sons of the king of the Isle of Avalon, which is now Glastenbury, and formerly in ancient times, a very magical place, the ancient home of the druids."

The boys asked the old man how he knew they were the sons of the king.

The old man said, "Everybody knows you boys are, Sir King William's sons. I did not live on the earth for thousands of years, passing through the ages and the sages of time, history, and time fulfillment of prophecy for being stupid. I promise you, young masters, even with my eyes closed in sleep, I can see, hear, and know everything since time began. For it is not for all of man to know what I have been sent to teach you now. For it is written in the scrolls of times of ancient past that two sons of the king would create world peace that would forever last."

The boys were in shock. They didn't know what to do or what to say. They packed their things and headed to the mountain while the old man led the way.

On the way to Mt. Preseli, the boys asked the ancient druid how he knew about the scrolls, and the old man said, "It was handed down to me by the leader of my order for the appointed day."

John asked the ancient mage, "What day is the appointed day?"

The druid said, "That day starts today."

Bill said, "Our parents don't even know that we are out here."

The ancient druid said, "I will contact your father myself. For what you now know that you didn't know, Sir King William needs to know himself. For one day, Master Bill, you are destined to and shall be king of all Britain."

When the boys and the ancient druid got to the other side of the mountain, they parted ways.

When the boys got back to the castle, their mother, Alyssa, was just given the highest award for the best fashion display at the club. She would be leaving to go home and cook the family some dinner. In the meantime, their father was just closing the all day long House of Commons meeting with the aristocrats and politicians about the treaty. About 40 percent said nay, and 60 percent said yay to the continued trust of the countries, including France. They all signed the new peace treaty under the United Nations' European Union to establish new and good foreign policy.

So when William was done with his kingly business and his political agenda, the king went home. Alyssa was just pulling her husband's dinner out of the woodstove, and the boys were preparing their clothes for school for the next day. But Bill was trying to decide if he wanted to continue to be homeschooled or if he wanted to for the first time in his life becomes a newly enrolled member and student in public school. The thought crossed his mind many times before, but it wasn't until he got older and lonelier that he realized that he had no friends being homeschooled. So the next morning after breakfast, all the boys except one went to school, and Sir King William and Queen Alyssa left. William went to work, and Alyssa went to London to see her parents. And Bill stayed home being tutored his school education. Before the tutor was done teaching, there was a knock on the door, and it was the leader of the Ancient Druid Order. Apparently, Bill and his brother John were required at Stonehenge for an official shaman coronation for the two brothers to become newly official members of the metaphysical school of the Ancient Order of the druids of Merlyn. And the tutor told the guests at the door that she would have to contact the boys' parents to get permission to release custody of the boys to the druids for apprenticeship. And the druids told the tutor that they already talked to the king outside the House of Commons, and he gave his approval. But if it made the tutor feel better about the discussion to go ahead and contact the parents. So the tutor sent word to the king via Pony Express, which nowadays is called the US Mail in America, and when the Pony Express got to its destination where the king was, the king walked right through the front door. And he said, "Why is Bill still here? John is already at Stonehenge as we speak."

And the tutor said, "I had to be sure, Your Majesty. For this is the first time I have seen these gentlemen, and I did not know if they were speaking the truth."

And William said, "They speak the truth. But because I'm so far away on a business trip, which is a part of my job as king, I could not get to you in time to tell you."

And the tutor said, "You got here in the nick of time, Sire."

So William paid the tutor for her teaching services and turned custody of his two sons, Bill and John, over to the druids for a twenty-year apprenticeship for the learning of the basic and advanced academics and for the teaching of the Ancient Wisdom and Powers of the ancient druids unto graduation. So the elder arch druid leaders of the Ancient Order waited until William was done with his business with the tutor and let Bill and John hug and kiss their parents and then took Bill and John to the Ancient University of the Ancient Order of the Druids of England, which is now called Glastenbury University of the United Kingdom. The king and queen was allowed to visit their sons on the weekends and the holidays. Bill and John would be in the druids college for the next twenty years, memorizing all the Ancient Wisdom because the druids did not allow the apprentices or students to write anything on parchment. This was a precautionary measure to prevent attempted theft of this special sacred secret knowledge. For it was forbidden to be taught to or learned by anyone who was not a student or druid or teacher and/or a bard of the Ancient Order itself. For those who violated the rules or revealed the Ancient Wisdom of the Ancient Order was put to death.

So after Sir King Williams III escorted his sons to the oldest and wisest university in the world, William went home in tears of joy. He knew that he and his wife and his other sons would miss them both days, weeks, and months. Years went by, and Bill and John grew into tall, handsome, and wise young men. They were fast, tough, and strong and highly intelligent and healthy as can be. By the time they reached their twentieth year in the druid college, they finally graduated. Their father and mother showed at their graduation at the college with their brothers, and they were so proud of Bill and John. The king threw the biggest graduation party in the history of all Europe. Everybody ate and drank and was merry. In the middle of the party, a troop scout of the lord marshal showed up and said, "France is coming with ten thousand legends of men."

And immediately, Sir King William III declared war. By the time the enemy's army got to the shores of England borders, it wasn't even France's army. It was Palestine. Apparently, some of the soldiers who fought in the last war was Muslim warriors, and Palestine wanted revenge for their dead. So King William and his army intercepted the Palestine army at the eastern border to fight when ten thousand druids showed up with Sir King William III's sons Bill and John, and Bill said, "Look behind me."

And lo and behold! It was the ancient old druid whose mystery name was really Merlyn the Magnificent. All the druids, including Merlyn, John, and Bill, formed Magical Circle. They lit the bonfires with the snap of their fingers real quick and invoked the Holy Spirit of the one true God of Israel and the Powers of the holy angels through the Magical Elements of earth, wind, water, and fire. For they spoke to the Lord of all flesh and spirits according to the ancient Magical Book of Enoch, and God, through Christ, did their desire.

All of a sudden, seven giant tornadoes appeared out of nowhere, and an earthquake so powerful came and was so strong it split the ground. And a thunderstorm came, and half of the enemy's army was swallowed up into the ground. One quarter of them was struck by lightning, and the other three quarters were blown away into the sea by the tornadoes. And that was the end of the enemies of Sir King William III of the isle of Avalon.

So seven years went by, and Bill Jr. was crowned the new king of the island of Avalon. And John was coronated as the new general of Sir King William IV's new army. And Bill married his new wife, who was also coronated William IV and England's new queen of Avalon. And her name was Alisha. And Bill and Alisha had seven children. And their names were Uriel, their firstborn; Raphiel, their second-born; Gabriel, their third-born; Lamiel, their fourth-born; Amiel, their fifth-born; Baraqiel, their sixth-born; and Joniel, their seventh-born. And all seven boys were named after the holy angels of God in heaven's angelic hierarchy. Young William was teaching his children how to fight and fence. Their mother, Alisha, was cooking breakfast. Uriel, Raphiel, Gabriel, Lamiel, Baraqiel, and Joniel were almost done with their fight and fencing lesson when their girlfriends arrived. Their dad told the boys to go ahead and take the rest of the day off. Alisha just got done making the boys' breakfast. The boys and the family ate breakfast for a whole hour with their girlfriends. When the family was done, Grandpa King William III and Alyssa went to the garden to go for a walk. Master Bill and Alisha went horseback riding. And the rest of the boys went fishing.

As the day slowly went by, the family came home for bed. William and Alyssa just came back from their nature walk through the garden. Bill Jr. and Alisha had also just returned from horseback riding. The rest of the brothers were still gone fishing. Alisha said, "Husband, has France made any improvements in their agreement with the constitution they signed in conjunction with the peace treaty they signed with other country leaders and with your father, William, the king of the Isle of Anglesey or in its old name in Welsh tongue, Avalon?"

William III said, "So far, so good, my queen. Everybody knows that actions speak louder than words."

Alisha said, "I just don't want your father's old political problems as ex-king of England to become yours or our children or grandchildren's problems."

King William said, "Worry not, my wife and queen, for everything is going as planned. For my father's work as ex-king of Avalon was not done in vain. For to worry unnecessarily about things that have already taken care of is to worry or despair for nothing. For the new peace treaty is being honored by all our allies."

Seven years went by, and the royal family lived in peace. Until one morning, during the celebration of the coronation of the new king of China, a messenger from Paris, France, came running into the palace and said, "Sire, the king of France requests your help in the northern territory to fight off the Muslims from India. They infiltrated the capitol and are now attempting to overthrow the French throne."

Sir King William IV declared war on India. The British troops marched and traveled three hundred miles to France by ships and raided Paris, France.

The war lasted for seven days, seven hours, seven minutes, and thirty-three seconds. By the time the war ended, all the Muslim terrorists were dead. King William and his armies traveled back to England.

By the time they came home, the British aristocrats, the rich barons, sirs, dukes of Windsor, and the commoners all cheered the soldiers as they came home. France was now finally freed from India's tyranny and attempted failed takeover. Thanks to the military backup support of King William IV's royal armies, France and England's foreign policy and relations as political allies under the European Union were now even stronger than ever.

That same night, Sir King William's family, friends, and people threw a celebration for the military success in killing off the Indian terrorists of the country of Hinduism.

Now that Bill was coronated as the new king of England as Sir King William IV, there would finally be peace in Britain, and his father, King William III could finally retire in peace and let his seventh son take over where he left off. Three more years went by, and all was good. Everybody went where they needed to go and did what they should.

Bill was the new king of Britain, and his brothers all graduated from Cambridge University. Their father had finally, after thirty-three years, stepped down from power as king of all England, as Sir King William III, before the succession of his seventh son, Bill.

All was calm in Europe for the first time in years. The family was enjoying a little game of horseback Polo. Grandfather, William III, was teaching his grandbabies how to walk, and the girls were being taught how to knit and crochet by their grandmother, Alyssa. The lord marshal and General O'Rieley of King William's high court showed up and said, "King John L. of Ireland has cordially invited the presence of Your Majesty, King William III and his son, the prince who has been officially coronated as the new king of England, to join Ireland for a honorary celebration for England and Ireland's victory. Victory over all the dictatorships and tyranny that led one third of Europe for so many centuries all the way back to the rule of the Roman Empire. This was before their fall by the Greeks in the Athens war when Alexander the Great was the new emperor of Rome, Italy, before the time of Jesus Christ."

Both William Sr. and his son, the new king, accepted. The lord marshal, Ben McKinsey, and General O'Rieley said, "We are headed back to Ireland tomorrow. We will tell King John L. of Ireland that Your Majesty, the old and new kings of England, have accepted his formal invitation. His Majesty of all the wee people of Kalarnie and the giants of Newgrange, who guard the land of the living dead, shall make formal arrangements for the royal family of Britain's arrival."

William III and his son, William IV, the new king, said, "Thank you, gentlemen. We will be there, and we shall be there on time."

The next morning came, and the lord marshal and the general traveled and back to London, England, and arrived back to Buckingham Palace at 7:30 a.m. They ate breakfast at the White Pony inn and had tea and crumpets by 8:00 a.m. They bathed, shaved, and brushed their teeth by 8:30 a.m., and they saw King John L. of

Ireland by 11:00 a.m. sharp. The lord marshal, Ben McKinsey, and General O'Rieley told King John I that they gave John's message to both Kings William III and IV, and the whole royal family of England would be at King John I's celebration party in Dublin, Ireland, on March 17 on the seventh hour in the afternoon in the year of our Lord AD 569. All the dukes, the barons, and the sirs connected to royalty, including many of the continental congressmen of the House of Commons would be there by the king's side. The wee people and the giants would be there, as well as the greatest wizard in the world who had lived thousands of years. He is the wizard who had heard and foreseen and fought every war in ancient times since the beginning of time, Merlyn the Magnificent. They would all be there for the greatest and most honorable celebration party of all time. They are the greatest kings and diplomats and soldiers and Magicians who live and who will ever live on God's green earth of good and evil.

So by 7:30 p.m., everybody gathered together at the giant long dinner table made of redwood sequoia and ancient oakwood. They prepared to eat at the feast of St. Patrick's Day to celebrate St. Patty's Day and to the independence of Ireland and England and France. They would all go down in ancient history as being others greatest allies for the first time. This was after many years of war and bloodshed. Many were initiated into the Knights Templar, who would later become the Freemasons society. Later, an evil French king had some Templars arrested, tried, and tortured and killed for crimes they did not commit on Friday the 13th. This is why Friday the 13th would for many years become a representation of bad luck. But for now England, Ireland, and France would become allies for many years, and they would live in peace. King John I of Ireland stood up and toasted all the allies. Sir King William III known as the conqueror and Sir King William IV, his son, for all the years, they successfully triumphed and had victory over all the enemies through all the year's wars. They lost many men in the process of keeping England free. And Sir King William IV stood up and toasted King John I, II, the Poetry King, and Merlyn the Magnificent, King John I and King William III and IV's headmaster, teacher and grandmaster mage for all the years of journeys and apprenticeship John I did before he was coronated king of Ireland, for also fighting and helping all the wee people of Ireland win the war against the evil magistrate, who was a steward of Ireland before John took Power over all of Ireland itself, when Merlyn and John I put the magistrates soldiers on their shelves. Just then, all the dukes, the barons, and continental congressman of the House of Commons and all the heads of states stood up and raised their glasses and said, "Here and salute and cheerio, mates."

When the success celebration of England and Ireland was over, both kings of Ireland and England turned around and toasted for France for making the most intelligent decision of France's life to call a truce with England, as once was an old military enemy, which was now one of Britain's greatest allies of all time next to Ireland, which was the greatest ally in the world. Along with Israel, which was the originator of the new Christian religion, the Christian stamped out paganism in many countries. Just then, Chancellor Shauntae Dupre and his ambassador of France stood up and toasted both Ireland and England for all the political and economical and military campaign accomplishments, including all the allies, noblemen, military leaders and personnel and Sir King John L. of Ireland and Sirs Kings William III and IV for their hard-earned achievements and success as well. Just then, all the heads of states and their families, friends, employees, and political and economical and military representatives all stood up and toasted all who were in the room. They said, "Here and salute and cheerio, mates."

Now as time came and went by, England and Ireland discovered the words of some countries to be the truth and the words of other countries, like Iran, Palestine, and India, to be lies. The earth started to change. Once there was wastelands in deserts and chopped-down trees with hardly any rivers or lakes to the point where the world was becoming like a dying dog with mange. But now there are big beautiful forests, animals, birds, and beautiful big redwood and sequoia and cedar and giant ancient oak trees resprouting in the spring as the morning birds sing. The way it is now was much worse when the world was under a curse. But God has ended that curse, and Merlyn helped replant and replenish all that was lost and all that had died. Now it became the time of scripture to be fulfilled. No more despair and no more being killed. Sir King William IV and his wife, Queen Alisha, was tired and worn out from all the politics, war, and negotiations of the past as new leaders of Great Britain. So they decided to take their vacation while Sir King William III, king of England, and his wife, the queen of England, Queen Alyssa, stayed home and watched the baby grandchildren.

    This vacation was a long time coming. They decided to go to the United Colonies of British Parliament to meet General Washington, one of Sir King Williams IV's greatest military generals of England. Sir King William IV and his wife, Alisha, arrived in Washington, DC, at seven o'clock the next morning. They went to a breakfast party for diplomats just down the road from the White House located at 1600 Pennsylvania, Washington, DC, 20500. William ordered biscuits and gravy. Alisha ordered strawberry pancakes with whipped cream. They ate their breakfast for one hour and a half. Then they paid for the food and left a tip on the table, and then they left to go meet General Washington, who was in charge of British intelligence and British military tactics and techniques. They arrived at the White House at 8:35 a.m. on a Friday. William and Alisha walked into the front gate and showed their credentials and IDs to the guards at the entrance. The guards showed the credentials to the secretary of state, and the secretary of state showed the credentials and IDs to the speaker of the house, and in turn, the speaker of the house showed the credentials to General Washington. The general said, "Let them in."

    So the guards let them in, and the maids took William's and his wife's coats and hats and put them in the presidential closet. Just then, the speaker of the house said, "General Washington is ready to see you, Your Majesty."

    And everybody stood to their feet and applauded when they saw General Washington walk through the back door as he headed toward the briefing room. This was where Sir King William IV and his wife, Queen Alisha, were sitting. General Washington said, "Greetings and welcome to the Oval Office of the White House, gentlemen."

    Just then, William and Alisha stood to their feet with thirty other diplomats and thirty-thee reporters. George confronted William, and his wife shook the president's hand. And George kissed Alisha's hand and said, "Welcome, friends and allies of Great Britain."

William said, "It's a great pleasure and honor to meet you, sir."

George said, "Have some seats, my friends."

Just then, the maids brought some English coffee and tea with crumpets while George and his cabinet members ate continental breakfast. The president said, "How have you been? It's a great pleasure and honor to meet you, my friends."

William and Alisha said, "Likewise, Mr. President."

The president said, "There are no formalities here, my friends. You can just call me George."

The leaders of the other countries stood up and said, "We are delighted to meet you, Mr. President. It's an honor and a pleasure to be here in this wonderful, beautiful, crisp morning."

George said, "Yes, it is, gentlemen, and welcome to the White House to you as well, my friends and colleagues. Have a seat."

William, Alisha, and the leaders of other countries all sat down at the same time.

"Mr. President, if I may speak freely," Sir William said.

"You may," George said. "You do so much better of a job, handling your job as king and your beautiful wife as queen and leaders of our mother country than King George ever did when he was king of Great Britain."

William IV and his wife, Queen Alisha, said, "We are sure that King George did the very best he could. At the same time. Thank you very much, George. Like many kings before me, as well as my father, the ex-king of England, King William III, I do the very best I can, George."

George said, "Thank you. All of Great Britain and all of the United Kingdom thank you, Sire."

William said, "I'm just doing my job, just like you, George. I didn't even know that I was heir to the throne until I was seven years old."

George said, "My administration, army, and I are always at your service. We are always awaiting your orders."

King William IV said, "I thank you for that, sir. My administration, cabinet members, all of my armies, and I are always at your disposal, my friend. If you need us for anything, you have but to ask."

The first president of the United states said, "Thank you, sir, even more."

King William and Alisha stayed for a few more hours, then they got up out of their guest chairs, shook George Washington's hand, and departed. Right directly behind them were the other leaders of other countries.

Alisha and William visited an American museum called The Smithsonian Institute. Then they visited the US Library of Congress and Capitol Hill, where bills are vetoed or adopted and implemented and/or passed with the majority of votes by the republicans, democrats, and independents. These votes can be to increase the US economy, jobs, transportation, housing, education, and law enforcement. They can also vote to lower taxes, the federal deficit, inflation, and to create US grant money for young teenagers who just graduated high school and want to go to college, where they can receive hands-on training through apprenticeship which ever vocational school of their choosing.

Afterward, they decided to go home. King William and Alisha got back late in the evening that same day. The maids and their servants came out and welcomed the king and queen back home. Dinner was just cooked by the castle chef and was being put on the dinner table.

William said to Alisha, "Mmm. Does that aroma smell good, my queen"

Alisha said, "Yes, my husband. It smells fit for a king."

William IV said, "Fit for a queen too."

The butler took their coats and hats and put them on the rack next to the door. William asked the butler, head of hospitality, and house servants if they got any mail and if anyone came the while they were gone. The butler, Nigel, said, "No, sir. No one came while you and Queen Alisha were gone on business. However, you did get some mail, Sire." Nigel handed William his mail and retired for the rest of the day until the next morning by permission of the king and queen.

William and Alisha thanked Nigel for watching the castle and making sure the Royal Army and the most elite royal guards kept people, peasants, outlaws, vandals, and criminals off the property. This prevented possible future invasions while William and Alisha were on vacation to the United Colonies of Europe. The queen and king finished their dinner, flossed, brushed their teeth, took baths, then retired to bed before having to wake up and do business. Night came and went; the next morning had come. William had an appointment with the House of Commons, and his wife, Alisha, had an appointment with her hairstylist. Four hours went by, and Alisha just got done having her hair styled. Alisha paid her beautician and started walking home.

A bright flash exploded ten feet from where she was walking. When the smoke cleared, lo and behold! It was Merlyn the Magnificent. Alisha bowed and said, "Bless thee, sir."

Merlyn walked up and grabbed Alisha by her right arm and said, "Greetings, Queen Alisha. It's an honor and great pleasure to see you, ma'am. But you must never bow to anyone but God and His only begotten son, Christ, the Messiah and King of the Jews."

Alisha said, "I apologize, sir. I thought when you appeared in front of me the way you did with great flashing power that you were God or the Messiah."

Merlyn said, "I thank you, Your Majesty, for those great but confused words. I mean, no offense when I say confused. I know you are of sound mind. My appearances have been scaring mortals into confusion for thousands of years."

"What brings you here, Merlyn?" asked the queen.

Merlyn said, "Alisha, I have come to bear good tidings and concerned news. The concerned news is to tell King William IV that he did a fabulous job as king of all England, but many of his and England's problems could have been avoided if he would have asked for help."

"Help from who?" Alisha asked.

"Help from God, and help from me."

Alisha said, "We prayed to God, but He wouldn't help us, and you were nowhere to be found."

Merlyn said, "On the contrary, my lady, God in Christ would have helped you if you had faith and works. If he would have used his brain intelligently, God in Christ would have helped him and England more. If he would have done what should have been done, that which his father almost failed to do before William IV was even born."

Alisha said, "And what was that?"

Merlyn said, "To negotiate with the leaders more. Some of his men wouldn't have died in war protecting England and the throne from the Hindus and the Muslims."

Alisha told Merlyn, "My husband said he will not make the same mistake his father almost did. Nobody could have helped how many of William IV's soldiers died in war."

Merlyn said, "My lady, with all due respect, I know William isn't just anyone, but, ma'am, anyone can make those promises. No one can be 100 percent sure they can keep them. Not even William IV. Although I have complete faith in God in Christ and total confidence in William IV, not even I, the greatest, most famous, and most powerful shaman in the world, can be 100 percent sure. Do not despair, my queen. Each day has its own sufficiency in time. No one but I, God, and the spirits can 100 percent foretell a human's future. No matter what does or doesn't happen or tries to happen, I will always be by your side forever. This is to make sure that what went wrong in the ancient past with the ancient ancestors never happens again. Once again, my queen, I apologize for all the times you, William, and his father before him didn't think I was anywhere to be found. The truth is, all those times in the past when you, William, and all of England thought you were going to perish, and through all those times you, William, and his brothers came close to being killed, it was I and God through Christ who saved you."

Alisha broke down and cried. She said, "I'm sorry I doubted you and thought you didn't care in all those times we did not see you there. We did not know what to think." Alisha hugged Merlyn and said, "Thank you, sir."

Merlyn said, "I don't blame you for being doubtful and scared. You are only so human. In any case, for any face, you are welcome, my queen, for you are loving, understanding, and fair."

Alisha said, "Thank you, Merlyn."

The old druid said, "You're welcome, my queen. I'll let you go for now because I know you have duties at home waiting."

Alisha said, "You're right, Merlyn. Thank you for taking time to talk to me."

Merlyn said, "As usual, my lady. It was an honor and a pleasure."

Lightning came out of the sky and struck the ground next to him. Merlyn the Magnificent disappeared into thin air.

Alisha went home and cooked dinner, and King William IV just walked through the front door and said, "My queen, I'm home!"

Alisha was just taking the cast iron Crock-Pot out of the woodstove. Alisha said, "I'm here, my love."

William opened up the kitchen doors, came in, wrapped his arms around Alisha, and gave her great big hug. He said, "Hello, my sweet. How have you been? How was your day?"

Alisha told her husband about the conversation she had with Merlyn the Magnificent and everything they both said, as well as how he appeared in front of her when they first met and how he disappeared into thin air after they were through talking. King William IV was impressed. Her husband said, "It sounds Merlyn was trying to get to know you and give you some concerned advice for me to improve my strategy, tactics, and techniques for future possible but not inevitable war. He needs not to worry for I have consulted with expert politicians and businessmen about strategic negotiations for future more improved foreign policy. I have been secretly studying psychology, sociology, and public relations to increase my education of Great Britain, the United Kingdom."

Alisha said, "Really, my love? I did not know. Before you graduate, congratulations, my husband. I now love you even more."

William hugged and kissed Alisha and said, "Thank you, my wife and queen. I would still love you even if you didn't congratulate me because I love you even more."

Alisha put some food from the Crock-Pot into William's plate and said, "I'll have your wine for you, my husband, with some ice-cold tea in just a moment."

William said, "It smells great, my love, as usual. It's probably just as delicious as it smells."

William and Alisha ate for an hour, went to the bathroom, took baths, flossed and brushed their teeth, put on deodorant, put on their pajamas, and went to bed. Night left, and morning came. It was a beautiful day just the same.

When William and Alisha were shutting their eyes to go to sleep for the rest of the night, all of the sudden, *kapow!* A loud noise was heard, and a bright Light flashed before their eyes. Lo and behold, it was Merlyn once again. William said, "What can we do for you, Merlyn?"

Merlyn said, "I humbly apologize to you, my king and queen, but I forgot to give my good tidings to Alisha in our last conversation before she left. We had finished talking about concerned news of you and your father's past."

William said, "And what is that, Merlyn?"

Merlyn said, "You and Alisha will have another son. His name will be Ariel. He will be named after the archangel Ariel, the angel of wisdom. He will rule the British Parliament throne through three generations. He will go down in European history as one of the greatest kings and shamans in the world."

William IV and Alisha paused for a moment and then asked, "When?"

Merlyn said, "You will know when after you make love on the altar stone of Stonehenge in Salisbury Plain on June 21, the longest day of the year. Great Britain will be one of the biggest, wisest, richest, and most powerful countries of all time."

Merlyn then said, "God bless you, my king and queen. Sleep well."

Merlyn the Magnificent disappeared into thin air.

William and Alisha slept for nine hours, woke up, and Alisha said, "Husband, we need to go get the children from their grandparents, King William III and your mother, Alyssa."

William IV said, "I hear you, my love, and I will. Just give me a chance to get up and make some coffee, pancakes, and eggs for breakfast, with melted butter and molasses syrup."

Alisha said, "Okay, my love, I will."

William got up, made coffee, cooked breakfast, and they both ate, drank their English coffee, and got dressed. They left to King William III's castle to get their children. William arrived at his father's house. He had tea and ate some crumpets. William IV stayed for about an hour. He got his kids, kissed his mother, and they left. Apparently, William IV's brother, Peter, and his wife, William IV's sister-in-law, were in town and at William III's castle, visiting. William IV didn't want to stay very long, thinking he would be intruding on his father's company, so he left.

When William IV arrived home an hour and a half later, his brothers, Simon, Philip, Ralph, George, and John, were sat down in the guest room dressed in royal formal attire. They all said, "Hail the king! Hello, Brother Bill."

William IV said, "Hello, my brothers! It is good to see you. It has been a long time. What brings you here this beautiful, crisp morning? What new has been happening in your lives since I saw you last?"

William IV's brothers said, "We were all invited to our college class reunion. We were wondering if you wanted to go?"

William IV said, "I would love to, Brothers, but I will have to notify my wife, Alisha, first."

"All right, Bill, we'll wait."

William said, "I'll be right back."

William went to Alisha, who was just pulling her children's lunch out of the woodstove. William told Alisha what his brothers told him. Alisha said, "Go if you want, my love, and have fun."

William IV hugged and kissed his wife. He changed clothes into his formal attire and left with his brothers to go to their college class reunion.

When the brothers arrived at their destination, they showed the security guard outside the college their invitations. As soon as they walked in the door, every professor, the dean of faculty, the ex-professors, all the old and new students bowed when William's present House of Commons speaker and duke of Windsor said with a loud voice, "Hail the king!" At that moment, everyone stood up, smiled, and shook one another's hand. All of a sudden, someone who William grew up with and went to the same school as his showed up. Her name was Vanessa. The first face she saw was William's. William IV said, "Long time no see, Vanessa. How have you been? How has life been treating you?"

Vanessa said, "I am married to the baron of Romania. I traveled around the world three times. I have three children and one on the way. I live in Count Dagon's old castle that baron bought for ten thousand pounds."

William said, "Congratulations, madam, for you have done well for yourself. What do you think of this reunion?"

Vanessa said, "I was debating on whether or not I even wanted to come."

William said, "Why is that?"

Vanessa said, "When I went to this college, when you did years ago, no one but you was nice to me because I was fat. Now that I am skinny and did modeling for many years, if it wasn't for me marrying the baron, every mean pervert here would want me now."

Bill said, "You should have said something back then, and I would have told my father, King William III, who was king of all England. He would have talked to these students' parents about their children's behavior, and those who were mean to you would have never bothered you again."

Vanessa said, "I was so upset back then and embarrassed. I didn't have the nerve to ask anybody anything, let alone help."

Bill said, "I know we only dated in the past and ended up marrying other people, but we are still friends. At the same time, if you would have come to me years ago when all this was happening, I promise you, my friend, I would have put a stop to your persecution a long time ago."

Vanessa said, "I thank you, Sire, for those warm sentiments. I handled it my own way."

Bill asked, "How was that?"

Vanessa said, "My family and I moved."

King William IV told Vanessa, "Point these people out to me right now, and justice will be done!"

Vanessa said, "I don't want a bad reputation for messing up the reunion."

William said, "When I'm done with these people, they will pay you five thousand pounds each for all the years of trouble and persecution they caused you. If they don't pay, they will die!"

Vanessa pointed her finger at one man whose name was James, the second was Damien, the third one was Gene. She also pointed out their girlfriends, Florence, Yolanda, Ruth, and Gina. The king suddenly stood up and pointed to all of the ex-students of Cambridge University, who persecuted Vanessa all those years ago, and called out their names individually and said, "It has come to my attention, according to Vanessa, that years ago when we all went to this same college, you persecuted Vanessa O'Reily! Not that it matters that she is related to royal Irish decent. Because what you did was so bad, she almost committed suicide. For this, on this Wednesday, in the year of our Lord, I am ordering you all to pay Vanessa five thousand pounds each for all the years you persecuted her, knocked her around, spit on her, and called her terrible names. If you don't, you will be arrested and executed tomorrow morning."

All of Vanessa's persecutors apologized and paid her money right on the spot. By the time Vanessa was paid, she received a total of thirty-five thousand pounds. Vanessa was so happy. She hugged and kissed King William IV and said, "Thank you, Sire."

She went back to the party where the table with the food and intoxicated punch was to fill her glass and drink. In the meantime, the ex-students who persecuted Vanessa picked up their stuff and left. The brothers stayed a few more hours and left.

By the time the boys got home, they were so tired. They almost passed out before they even walked in the door. King William IV told his brothers, "Thanks, mates, for the great time at the class reunion. I really enjoyed myself. We all need to get outdoors more and spend more time together."

The brothers said, "You're welcome, Brother King. You're right, we do. However, we all have so many responsibilities and obligations that consume most of our schedule time. We sometimes, and lately most of the time, don't even have time for ourselves. When we do, we try to spend it with you and your family and with our own."

William said, "Yes, my brothers, I understand. If we waste all our precious God-given time doing nothing but working for a living, even though there is still work to do and a lot of it to get done, life will slip right by us as the years come and go. So next time, we will plan ahead of time to get together and spend some quality time together as a family."

The brothers agreed and proceeded to get up out of their chairs and hug their brother, the king. They walked out of the castle doors and said, "We love you, Brother William."

William said, "I love you too, my brothers. Be careful going home. Thanks once again and Godspeed."

King William decided to turn in for the rest of the night. Alisha was just pulling the cast iron pot out of the woodstove oven. William said, "Mmmm. That smells good. What is it?"

Alisha said, "It is your favorite, my love. It's venison stew. I shot it myself this morning after you left. I added potatoes, onions, peppers, carrots, mushrooms, tomatoes, herbs, spices, and honey. It's all cooked in red and white wine and butter."

William said, "Surely, my queen, you have outdone yourself. You did not have to do all this for me."

Alisha said, "I did it all because I love you, my husband. I wanted my food that I cooked to be fit for a king. After all, my love, you are not just my husband, you are the king."

Sir William IV said, "Thank you, my love. I owe you a great deal."

Alisha said, "William, our marriage is not a business deal or business arrangement like the ones you and the other heads of states make at the House of Commons! I am your wife and queen of all England. It's my duty under the law and under God to clean and cook for you."

William said, "Thank you, my love. You are right once again."

William IV and Alisha were just about to turn in for the night when suddenly there was a knock at the door. When William opened it, it was Sir Winston Sinclair, who originally attended William III's first meeting with the heads of states.

King William IV asked, "Sir Winston, what can I do for you?"

Sir Winston Sinclair said, "Sire, I am sorry to disturb you at this time of night, but I heard from one of our military scouts. He said that the Saxons are planning an attack on castle grounds when everyone goes to sleep."

William asked, "How does this scout know this for sure?"

Winston said, "He overheard the Saxon king telling his generals and men at arms what I am telling you now."

King William IV declared war on the Saxons. William ordered his men to make traps all around the castle, to fill the mote with flammable oil, and to have torches burning and ready to be dropped into the mote by the general's order. He also ordered to camouflage the traps and dig holes all around the castle property. He put his assassins in the body holes and camouflaged them. He said to use the secret art of the element of surprise and to get the special force militia to come as backup while the castle army guards the throne. After all the preparations were made and done, Sir King William and his army personal guard and militia and special forces waited. Seven hours went by, and there were no Saxons in sight. Right when William IV and his men thought that Sir Winston Sinclair's massage was a lie and they were about to give up waiting, loud screaming came from the south wing of the castle property perimeter. Apparently, the Saxons tried a sneak attack on the south side of royal land and were starting to be killed by the assassins camouflaged in the ground. By the time they first heard the noise, half of the Saxon warriors were three-fourths of the way to the castle. Then the all-out full-fledged battle began.

It was a bloody one, and the battle lasted a whole three hours and seven minutes. When the war was over, Sir King William's men were not injured nor perished. However, every single Saxon on the battlefield was dead. Just when they all thought the war was over with, here came ten thousand Vikings from the east direction. Sir King William IV, all his family, and men thought they were about to be outnumbered and killed. Out of nowhere, Sir King John L. of Ireland showed up with Merlyn and all his men. While Sir King John L. of Ireland was helping Sir King William IV and his army kill off half of the Vikings, Merlyn, John, and Bill raised their magical staffs and conjured the holy angels of heaven, Gabriel, Raphiel. and Michael. The holy angels raised their hands in the air, and fire and lightning shot from their fingers, killing the rest of the Vikings.

When the war was finally over with, Sir King William IV and Sir John L. of Ireland shook hands. Everybody helped one another stand on their feet, hugged, and shook each other's hands. After getting cleaned up and wounds treated, they all went to Sir King William IV's castle and ate the biggest dinner Queen Alisha ever cooked in her entire life. They celebrated England and Ireland's victory, winning the biggest war England and Ireland ever fought against the Anglo-Saxons and the Vikings in the history of both countries.

After the celebration was over, everyone went home. King William IV wrote some poetry for his family to always remember him by. It was written like this:

> I am King William IV, my father was III, and I am king of all England as you have heard. Life as a king was good and bad. Yet we never gave up, and we fought for everything we had. We never lost a war that we did fight because with Merlyn's help in Christ, we had help from the king of Ireland and from the Lord of all flesh and spirits, and we conquered our enemy with all of Almighty God's might! So as I write these poems for all to read, know that I did the best I could as your king. I write poems as the sun rises and as the morning birds sing.
>
> So live and let live in peace and love one another as God, Jesus, Merlyn, King John L. of Ireland, and I, Sir King William IV, has loved you enough to risk all our lives to fight many wars like our ancient ancestors did in ancient times before.

And know that we are all free as the holy angels
of the Lord God of Israel spread their wings!

Many, many, more years went by, and they all lived happily ever after.
Until the next story!

About the Author

The author has been writing stories since he was nine years old, and for over forty years, he has studied the homeopathic holistic alternative shaman herbal medication and has been a practicing magus in art, scholarship, poetry, writing, music, and high arcane and Divine Magic his whole life, a jack-of-all-trades and a master of them all. For nothing could confine his spirit, not even the *wall!*

CPSIA information can be obtained
at www.ICGtesting.com
Printed in the USA
BVHW032016070619
550498BV00001B/22/P